100

REASONS

TO LOVE

AUDREY

HEPBURN

100 REASONS TO LOVE AUDREY HEPBURN

JOANNA BENECKE

PLEXUS, LONDON

'I believe in pink.
I believe that laughing
is the best calorie burner.
I believe in kissing,
kissing a lot.
I believe in being strong when
everything seems to be going wrong.
I believe that happy girls
are the prettiest girls.
I believe that tomorrow is another day
and I believe in miracles.'
Audrey Hepburn

'For beautiful eyes, look for the good in others; for beautiful lips, speak only words of kindness; and for poise, walk with the knowledge that you are never alone.'
Audrey Hepburn

1. She gave the world the Little Black Dress

In a 2010 survey conducted by LOVEFiLM, Audrey's little black number from *Breakfast at Tiffany's* was chosen as the best dress ever worn by a woman in a film. Tailored to flatter Audrey's sylph-like frame to perfection – by Hubert de Givenchy, the legendary French designer who loved Audrey like a 'sister' – this satin creation is the ultimate in timeless chic. Teamed with a classic up-do, string of pearls and cigarette holder, the iconic ensemble seems so perfectly organic now, but did you know that Givenchy's daring original design (with a slit open all the way to Audrey's thigh) had to be tempered by doyenne of costume designers, Edith Head, at Paramount's request?

2. The same LBD that raised almost a million dollars for charity

After Hepburn's death in 1993, Givenchy donated her black satin gown to City of Joy Aid. The charity waited till 2006 to auction it off at Christie's for more than $900,000! The money helped build a school in Calcutta, a project UNICEF-worker Audrey would have supported whole-heartedly.

3. She had a pet deer named Pippin (Ip for short)

The doe-eyed lookalikes met on the set of *Green Mansions* back in 1959 and took the idea of pets resembling their owners to a whole new level. As Audrey was playing a girl living in the Venezuelan jungle, who has a strong connection to a fawn who follows her everywhere, one of the animal trainers suggested she take little Pippin home with her for bonding purposes. Bonding definitely ensued! Before long, the two were inseparable. Affectionate Ip loved nothing better than to curl up next to Audrey as she slept. The baby deer became an important part of the family and was even treated to a custom-made bathtub. 'It was truly amazing to see Audrey with that fawn,' writes Bob Willoughby in *Remembering Audrey*. 'While Audrey's maid had been told about the little deer, she could not believe her eyes seeing Ip sleeping with Audrey so calmly. She was shaking her head and just kept smiling.' And – frankly – who wouldn't? An internet search reveals several heart-warming snaps of these dears together . . . it's damn near impossible to say who's cuter.

4. She was an accomplished linguist

Call it what you will – *amour, liefde, amor, amore* – Audrey's passion for languages knew no bounds. Born to a British father and a Dutch mother, the globe-travelling polyglot spoke not only English and Dutch, but also French, Spanish and Italian.

5. She overcame childhood trauma

Born Audrey Kathleen Ruston in Brussels on 4 May 1929, Audrey spent her first
years moving between Belgium, England and Holland. Her parents' marriage broke
down in the mid-1930s and her father, Joseph Victor Anthony Ruston, deserted the
family, leaving no forwarding address (Audrey referred to this as 'the most traumatic
event of my life'). Her mother, Baroness Ella van Heemstra, moved Audrey to Kent,
placing her in a tiny independent school in Elham. With Europe on the verge of
war, Ella made the decision to leave England for Holland, believing they would be
safer there, as the Netherlands had been neutral during World War One. Little did
she know that this move would entail years of suffering during the Nazi occupation
which would see several of Audrey's friends and relations deported or killed,
including her uncle who was executed in the street.

6. She helped fight the Nazis

Although her parents, especially her father, allegedly had some rather unsavoury Nazi-sympathetic views, their daughter did not share them. Though still very young during the war, Audrey performed in ballet recitals and donated the money she earned to the Resistance movement. She also occasionally acted as a courier, delivering money and papers from one Resistance worker to another.

7. She knew the value of freedom

Having narrowly escaped being rounded up by Nazis looking for Dutch girls to work in their kitchens, Audrey recalled the joy of liberation at the end of the war: 'it's something that's very hard to verbalise. Freedom is more like something in the air. For me, it was hearing soldiers speaking English instead of German, and smelling real tobacco smoke again from their cigarettes.' She remained a lifelong smoker who always preferred British cigarettes.

8. She shared her experiences of war

Speaking of the war years, Audrey told the *Sunday Telegraph* in 1991, 'I have memories. More than once I was at the station seeing trainloads of Jews being transported, seeing all these faces over the top of the wagon. I remember, very sharply, one little boy standing with his parents on the platform, very pale, very blond, wearing a coat that was much too big for him, and he stepped on to the train. I was a child observing a child.' She also recalled being told to hide her Britishness. 'My mother was worried about [my] speaking English in the streets with Germans all around.'

9. And continued to speak out against the Nazis

'We saw young men put against the wall and shot, and they'd close the street and then open it and you could pass by again . . . Don't discount anything awful you hear or read about the Nazis. It's worse than you could ever imagine.'

10. She understood how starving children felt

During the unthinkably harsh 'Hunger Winter' of 1944, when the Nazis cut off food supplies to the Dutch, Audrey nearly starved to death, but survived by foraging for tulip bulbs and other plants. 'We ate nettles and everyone tried to boil grass – in addition to tulips,' she said. At the end of the war, aged sixteen, Audrey weighed just 88 pounds and was suffering from jaundice, asthma and anaemia. Her years of malnutrition would lead to health problems throughout her adult life. She always struggled to put on weight, no matter how much she ate, and consequently attracted – totally untrue – rumours of an eating disorder.

11. She never stopped caring about UNICEF

Audrey never forgot what it was to go hungry and wanted to help other youngsters in similarly dire situations around the globe. 'I can testify to what UNICEF means to children,' she explained, 'because I was among those who received food and medical relief right after World War Two'. In 1988, she was appointed a UNICEF Special Ambassador for her tireless humanitarian efforts. And Audrey's charitable legacy didn't end there. The following year, she became one of the charity's Goodwill Ambassadors. Unveiled in 2002, a beautiful bronze statuette, entitled 'The Spirit of Audrey', stands outside UNICEF HQ in New York: a lasting reminder of one of the most beautiful souls in Hollywood.

12. She has her very own breed of

tulip

Audrey loved gardening – and botanists love Audrey! First cultivated in Holland in 1990, the Audrey Hepburn tulip is snowy white, long-necked and graceful, just like the lady herself. So the young girl who was forced to eat tulips to save herself from starvation grew up to have a tulip named after her – blooming wonderful!

13. Without Audrey, there'd be no 'Moon River'

The sweet and simple melody sung by Audrey as Holly Golightly in *Breakfast at Tiffany's* sounds like it was penned especially for her. And that's because it was. Composer Henry Mancini tailored the song to match her vocal range exactly. 'No one else ever understood it so completely,' mused the Hollywood maestro. 'There have been more than a thousand versions of "Moon River", but hers is unquestionably the greatest.'

...her mother
was a baroness

Always convincing as on-screen royalty, Audrey had more than a little aristocratic blood coursing through her veins. Her mother, Baroness Ella van Heemstra, was the third daughter of Baron Aarnoud van Heemstra, sometime Mayor of Arnhem in the Netherlands. The van Heemstras even had a family crest in the shape of a golden eagle.

15. She put Givenchy on the fashion map

When taciturn young designer Hubert de Givenchy was called to the set of *Sabrina* in 1953, he was in for a surprise. He was expecting to meet the formidable actress Katharine Hepburn, not the gamine Mademoiselle Audrey (just two years older than Givenchy himself). But Givenchy definitely wasn't disappointed. In an interview with the *Wall Street Journal*, the couture king described their first encounter. 'She was ravishing. But she was dressed in a way that surprised me: small pants, ballerina flats. I asked myself, "Who is this young lady?" We liked each other immediately.'

16. She stuck up for her friends

Givenchy continues, 'We made the dresses [for *Sabrina*]. The film came out. It won an Oscar for the dresses but I didn't get any credit. [The Academy Award went to the official costume designer, Edith Head.] Audrey was furious. She demanded, "Each time I'm in a film, Givenchy dresses me."' So began the classiest association in cinematic costumier history! Up to the very end of her life, Audrey remained convinced that, 'His are the only clothes in which I am myself. He is far more than a couturier; he is a creator of personality.' The two had such a connection that a grief-stricken Givenchy even helped carry Audrey's coffin through the church at her funeral.

17. She nearly missed Breakfast (at Tiffany's)

As far as author Truman Capote was concerned, Marilyn Monroe – with her voluptuous figure, platinum locks and obvious bombshell credentials – was the only choice to play Holly Golightly in *Breakfast at Tiffany's*. But rumour has it that Marilyn turned down the role at the last minute, concerned that playing a 'lady of the night' would harm her reputation (either that or you can blame it on contractual issues). Fortunately, Audrey was on hand to fill Holly's kitten heels, despite the vocal disapproval of Capote himself. 'Paramount double-crossed me and cast Audrey,' the disgruntled author is reported to have griped. But what a different film it would have been without Ms Hepburn's unique blend of otherworldly beauty and childlike naivety! The actress's classy presence – so at odds with the tawdriness of Holly's life – creates a fascinatingly complex character: incandescent, indefinable and truly iconic. (NB, Audrey could never be tawdry.)

18. Audrey loved chocolate – and wasn't afraid to admit it

Sweet-toothed Audrey was a firm believer in 'everything in moderation'. Each night before curling up with little Ip, she'd treat herself to a square or two of cooking chocolate (dark not milky – despite the fact that Audrey's computer-generated image recently appeared in a UK ad for Galaxy milk chocolate).

19. She had her cake and ate it

'Let's face it,' Audrey once stated, 'a nice creamy chocolate cake does a lot for a lot of people. It does for me.'

20. But she always knew when to stop

Though not much of a snacker (by her own admission), Audrey did eat heartily at meal times. 'I eat everything, *everything*,' the svelte starlet asserted. 'But as soon as I'm satisfied, a little hatch closes and I stop.'

21. She was never a diva

No one who worked with Audrey ever had a bad word to say about her. In *Enchanted: the Life of Audrey Hepburn*, Donald Spoto describes her as humble, polite, undemanding and respectful of all cast and crew members. Audrey's second son Luca Dotti describes his mother's charming work ethic: 'throughout her life she rose at dawn, a habit formed when she had to arrive on time to a set looking perfect and knowing her lines by heart'.

22. Her smile

Radiant Audrey – especially as *Roman Holiday*'s spirited princess-on-the-run – was living proof of what she always believed: 'happy girls are the prettiest girls'.

23. She had a Yorkshire terrier named
Mr Famous

Before celebrity lap-dogs became the vogue, there was Audrey's beloved Yorkie, Mr Famous. The object of his mistress's adoration, Mr Famous appeared alongside Audrey on several glossy magazine covers, as well as making a cameo appearance in 1957's *Funny Face*. Sadly, he was knocked down by a car on Wiltshire Boulevard while Audrey was filming *The Children's Hour* in 1961, but she never forgot her devoted companion. Animals continued to be an important part of her life; she had four Jack Russell terriers with her final partner, Robert Wolders.

24. She loved unusual roles

Hollywood legend has it that Ingrid Bergman suggested Audrey for the lead in *The Nun's Story* – and what a good job she did, as the part proved to be one of Audrey's favourites. She plays Sister Luke, a Belgian woman who enters a convent and travels to the Congo to care for the sick. As someone who valued charity work deeply, no wonder this role spoke to Audrey. Filming was arduous and included time on location in a leper colony in the Congo. The movie, which the studio never expected to be a hit, ended up being a huge critical success – and Warner Bros' highest grossing picture of 1959.

25. She was the epitome of understated style

Think you need flesh-flashing gowns and copious amounts of bling to steal the spotlight? Think again. Audrey eschewed the bombshell tactics of her attention-grabbing contemporaries in favour of strong clean lines, bold blocks of colour and quirky statement pieces (a bow-tie here, a conical straw hat there) to create a strikingly simple signature look that was all her own.

26. She gave us all the freedom
to wear flats

Audrey's dainty ballet pumps not only caught Givenchy's eye, but caused quite a stir in an era of sky-high Hollywood heels . . . and women across the world breathed a sigh of relief! Equal parts pretty and practical, these slip-on shoes are the last word in comfortable chic. They are now a modern-day wardrobe staple – all because of Ms Hepburn.

27. She's the original poster girl for

inner beauty

Pretty, witty Audrey may have been one of the most naturally beautiful women ever to grace the planet, but she never took her looks too seriously. 'Make-up can only make you look pretty on the outside, but it doesn't help if you're ugly on the inside. Unless you eat the make-up,' she quipped. She believed that: 'the beauty of a woman is not in a facial mole, but . . . reflected in her soul. It is the caring that she lovingly gives, the passion that she knows.'

28. She joked about her appearance

Despite being one of the most admired beauties of all time, Audrey kept both ballet pumps firmly on the ground. Her son Sean Ferrer explained that she used to tell him, 'I'm fake thin. Don't tell anyone.'

29. And believed her looks were attainable by everyone

In an interview with Barbara Walters just before Audrey's sixtieth birthday, the ever-gorgeous actress-turned-charity-worker claimed her appearance 'appeals more to women than to men'. She believed the reason for this was that she created 'an attainable look' which others could embrace. 'You can look like Audrey Hepburn,' she exclaimed, 'by piling up the hair, buying the large glasses, wearing the little sleeveless dresses.' If only it were that simple . . .

30. She merged charm with determined discipline

The value of Audrey's early devotion to dance was not lost on Humphrey Bogart – who played Audrey's sedate-but-smitten love interest in *Sabrina*. 'She's disciplined,' he drawled, 'like all those ballet dames.'

31. She knew the importance of alone-time

As much as she loved her family and friends, Audrey was a bit of an introvert and definitely appreciated the value of me-time. 'I love being by myself,' the sought-after starlet revealed. 'I love being outdoors, love taking a long walk with my dogs and looking at the trees, flowers, the sky . . . I don't want to be alone – I want to be left alone.'

32. She was truly, madly, deeply
in love with Paris

Like many of the characters she played onscreen –
think *Funny Face*'s Jo running rings around the Arc
de Triomphe, or descending the sweeping marble
staircase of the majestic opera house – Audrey
couldn't resist the lure of France's magical capital
city. As she herself put it, 'Paris is always a good idea.'

33. She felt safe in Switzerland

In his 2005 biography of his mother, Sean Ferrer describes how Audrey valued the peace and security offered by Switzerland, that European bastion of neutrality, a place where she could lead a normal life without being hounded by photographers. In 1996, three years after her death, the Audrey Hepburn Pavilion opened in a converted schoolhouse in Tolochenaz near where she had lived on and off for thirty years. By the time the museum closed its doors in 2002 – the items on display had been loaned by Audrey's sons on a temporary basis only – it had received almost 30,000 visitors from around the world and raised $276,000 for children's charities.

34. But her heart belonged to Rome

In *Roman Holiday*, when asked 'Which of the cities visited did Your Highness enjoy the most?' Audrey's character replies, 'Rome! By all means, Rome . . .' which wouldn't have required much acting. In his book *Audrey in Rome*, Luca Dotti explores his mother's longstanding love affair with the Eternal City (it was her home for almost twenty years), explaining that her connection with Rome influenced her deeply and that 'her image evolved to include characteristics of the Roman spirit'.

35. And Rome loved her back

With the success of *Roman Holiday*, a hopeful breath of fresh air in the post-war gloom, Audrey 'became almost a second Colosseum: an icon of the city, an icon of a different, free-and-easy Roman spirit that was symbolised by a girl who travelled the world on a Vespa,' writes Luca Dotti. Over the years, Audrey was increasingly drawn to the Italian capital, creating a home there in the 1960s. In turn, Luca watched Rome embrace his beloved mamma. 'Rome always protected my mother, giving her time and space,' he said.

36. She didn't let anything get in the way of her charity work

Despite being diagnosed with the rare form of cancer which would eventually kill her, Audrey went on more than fifty trips on behalf of UNICEF during the last five years of her life, visiting Sudan, El Salvador, Vietnam, Ethiopia and Somalia.

37. She resolutely refused to put herself first

What drove Audrey to continue with her exhausting UNICEF travels, even while she was battling cancer? Audrey's compulsion to care for others can be traced back to her altruistic mother, Baroness Ella van Heemstra, whose charity work included helping Vietnam War veterans in San Francisco. 'It's that wonderful old-fashioned idea that others come first and you come second,' explained Audrey. 'This was the whole ethic by which I was brought up. Others matter more than you do, so "don't fuss, dear; get on with it."'

38. She was 'too tall'

Online rumours abound that Audrey was five foot ten. This seems unlikely (unless all her co-stars were on stilts), but – at five foot six and a half – she *was* taller than most actresses of her time and her willowy frame and swanlike neck made her appear even statelier than she was. Being 'too tall' contributed to the end of her ballet dreams but, on the plus side, it meant she could get away with wearing those comfy flat shoes.

39. Dancing taught her the importance of hard work

After World War Two, Ella moved with Audrey, who was intent on being a ballerina, to Amsterdam. There, the teenager studied with the premier name in Dutch ballet, Sonia Gaskell. 'Sonia taught me that if you worked really hard, you'd succeed,' Audrey recalled, 'and that everything had to come from the inside.'

40. When her dreams were crushed, she moved on

After moving back to England, Audrey supported herself as a model so she could study at the prestigious Ballet Rambert in London. Her dreams came crashing down when she was told that, although she had talent, the malnutrition she had suffered as a child had weakened her constitution and this – combined with her height – meant she would never achieve her dream of becoming a prima ballerina. Rather than letting this news crush her, Audrey decided to concentrate on her acting.

41. 'Have they all gone?'

After being chosen as one of ten chorus girls from over 1,000 hopefuls, Audrey was given one solitary line in the 1948 show, *High Button Shoes.* Audrey asked, 'Have they all gone?' once a night for 291 performances.

42. Her humble chorus girl beginnings

Audrey's rise to fame is like something straight off the silver screen. With her mother working menial jobs to support the family, Audrey knew she had to find employment too. With her dancing background, looking for work as a chorus girl in the West End made sense. In her own words, 'I needed the money; it paid £3 more than ballet jobs.' After being spotted by a casting director, Audrey registered as a freelance film actress. You can glimpse an unknown Ms Hepburn in minor roles in the 1951 movies, *One Wild Oat*, *Laughter in Paradise*, *Young Wives' Tale* and *The Lavender Hill Mob*. She landed her first major supporting role in Thorold Dickinson's *Secret People* (1952), playing a ballerina (of course she performed all her own dance sequences). However, her first starring role was to be on the stage, not the screen . . .

43. She was the original Gigi

Long before Leslie Caron played the Parisian courtesan-in-training in Vincente Minnelli's film, Audrey owned the part on Broadway. As soon as the author Colette, on the hunt for a lead actress for the dramatised version of her novel, spotted Audrey she reportedly announced, 'Voilà! There's . . . Gigi!'

44. She was incredibly modest at the start of her career

When approached by Colette to star in *Gigi*, Audrey's response was characteristically self-deprecating. 'I wouldn't be able to, because I can't act.' Thankfully the writer insisted, Audrey relented, and her performance was a hit with audiences and critics alike, proving she definitely had the talent to carry a major stage show.

45. . . . . and at the end of it

'How shall I sum up my life? I think I've been particularly lucky.'

46. She picked her battles wisely

Known for her mild manner and gracious nature, on the occasions when Audrey did put her foot down, anyone with any sense knew to pay attention. Legend has it that when, after a preview screening of *Breakfast at Tiffany's*, Paramount exec Martin Rackin announced, '"Moonriver" has to go', Audrey responded with 'over my dead body'. Luckily, Rackin gave in and the song went on to win an Academy Award.

47. She was known as 'Princess'

But not in the spoilt, entitled sense of the word. This was back when royalty stood for old-school impeccable manners and self-sacrifice. Frank Sinatra bestowed the affectionate nickname on Audrey soon after their first meeting, recognising her perfect poise, manners and natural grace.

48. And had her big breakthrough
playing a princess

In 1953 Audrey landed her first leading role on-screen in *Roman Holiday* playing Princess Ann, a young royal keen to have a taste of 'real' life by escaping her entourage and going around Rome incognito. The quotation marks are necessary, as driving up the Pantheon on the back of Gregory Peck's Vespa is the sort of 'real' that only happens to Audrey. The director, William Wyler, had initially envisaged Elizabeth Taylor playing the role, but was so impressed by Audrey's screen test that he decided to take a pop on an unknown. He said, 'She had everything I was looking for: charm, innocence, and talent. She also was very funny. She was absolutely enchanting and we said, "That's the girl!"' Elementary, my dear Wyler.

49. But is equally well known as a cockney flower girl

Though the role of Eliza Doolittle had been played on stage by Julie Andrews, Audrey ended up landing the part in Warner Bros' 1964 celluloid version of *My Fair Lady*. Despite not being a musical theatre singer (most of her numbers were dubbed by singer Marni Nixon, much to Audrey's disappointment) and having a rather unique take on the East End accent, her performance is just so darn likeable that critics and audiences melted regardless.

50. She didn't steal Julie Andrews's part

In case you were wondering, Audrey didn't set out to nab Julie's role. Producer Jack L. Warner was keen to gather as many big names as possible for the movie and Julie was, at that time, a newcomer. Warner wanted Cary Grant to take on Rex Harrison's role of Professor Higgins to Audrey's Eliza. But Grant declined, saying that he wouldn't even go and see the film if Harrison wasn't playing Higgins! Of course kind-hearted Audrey said her role should go to Ms Andrews, but when the studio announced it would approach someone else entirely if Audrey turned Eliza down, she relented and became the 'bankable star' of the film. (Oh, and Julie wound up doing a little movie called *Mary Poppins* that year, so it all worked out rather supercalifragilisticexpialidociously.)

51. *That* little white dress

The figure-hugging floor-length high-necked frothy lace-fest, decorated with some form of black bunting, which Eliza wears to the races in *My Fair Lady* could easily have ended up looking like some strange avant-garde wilted meringue – but on Audrey it's a thing of extraordinary beauty! The creation came in at number six on LOVEFiLM's list of the most popular dresses in film history. It also topped the list of the most expensive movie memorabilia ever sold at auction. In 2011, the gown sold for a whopping $4.5million! Flippin' heck, as Ms Doolittle might say.

52. She knew what mattered
most in life

Having lost everything of material value during World War Two, Audrey was not overly attached to possessions. What mattered to her was people. 'The best thing to hold onto in life is each other,' she believed.

53. She loved to laugh

Can anyone resist Audrey's gorgeously contagious laugh? 'I love people who make me laugh,' she admitted. 'I honestly think it's the thing I love most – to laugh. It cures a multitude of ills. It's probably the most important thing in a person.'

54. She never
bought into
the celebrity hype

Perhaps because the hardship of her early years gave her a wider perspective on the world, or maybe because of her innate humility, Audrey never could understand the paparazzi – or their fascination with her personal life. 'There's never been a helluva lot to say about me,' she remarked.

55. She had her insecurities

Strange though it may seem, Audrey always thought her feet and her nose too big, proving that – no matter how beautiful – women are always their own harshest critics. Her son Luca explains, 'One of the reasons for her low self-esteem is that when she started out some newspaper articles depicted her as not so perfect. She had big feet [a US size 10], a big nose and small breasts. She wasn't at all what the average beautiful girl was perceived as, especially by men.'

56. But she knew sex appeal isn't about size

'Sex appeal is something that you feel deep down inside,' said Audrey. 'It's suggested rather than shown. I'm not as well-stacked as Sophia Loren or Gina Lollobrigida, but there is more to sex appeal than just measurements. I don't need a bedroom to prove my womanliness. I can convey just as much sex appeal picking apples off a tree or standing in the rain.'

57. She helped women

Though less of a vocal feminist than her namesake Katharine Hepburn, Audrey showed women that it was okay to look and be different. As the *New York Times* put it, 'What a burden she lifted from women. There was proof that looking good need not be synonymous with looking bimbo. Thanks to their first glimpse of Audrey Hepburn in *Roman Holiday*, half a generation of young females stopped stuffing their bras and teetering on stiletto heels.'

58. She can even make a TV commercial beautiful

Many Hepburn fans were startled — and not altogether pleased — to see a young Audrey appear in a recent TV advertisement for Galaxy chocolate bars. Was it really okay, they asked, to resurrect the lovely starlet for such a money-spinning scheme? On the plus side, the footage has been licensed by Audrey's sons, who are clearly best placed to guess at their mother's wishes. Quite possibly she would have been tickled by the idea of stealing a bus conductor's hat in order to commandeer a chauffeur and enjoy her snack in peace. After all, a chocoholic icon's gotta do what a chocoholic icon's gotta do.

59. She's still giving to charity

Audrey's good work carries on although she is no longer with us, thanks to the Audrey Hepburn Children's Fund, set up after her death by her sons and her partner, Robert Wolders, to keep her charitable legacy alive. The fund provides help and support to kids all over the world, 'with the health, well being and education of children as the central mission'. Every advertising campaign that uses Audrey's image must support the charity.

60. She overcame personal tragedy in adult life

Audrey's tragic losses were not confined to her childhood: during her first marriage, to Mel Ferrer, she suffered two miscarriages, one caused by the physical and emotional stress of falling from a horse on the Mexican set of John Huston's *The Unforgiven* in 1959, an accident which left her spine broken in four places. Once she'd recovered in hospital and worn a brace for a month, stoical Audrey returned to complete the movie. She then took a year out from movie-making and had her first child, Sean Hepburn Ferrer. She had another son, Luca Dotti, with her second husband, but suffered several more miscarriages throughout her life.

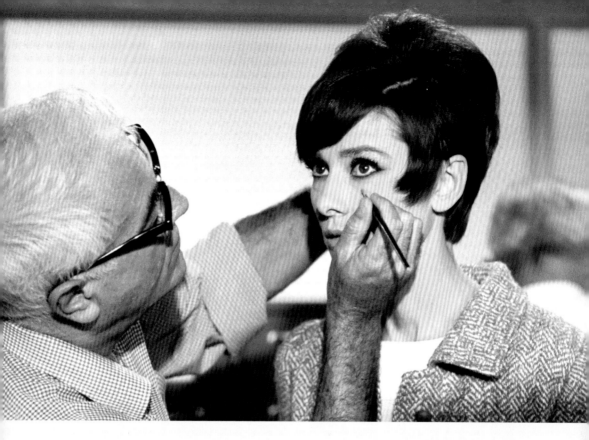

61. Her iconic eyes

Though Audrey was blessed with the most naturally gorgeous, kind, twinkly peepers, they were beautifully enhanced by her signature eye makeup. Her famous 'mascara look' and 'wing eyebrows' were designed by Alberto de Rossi, her Italian makeup artist. Audrey and Alberto loved working together and became lifelong friends.

62. Her sunglasses

The oversized 'Manhattan' shades worn by Audrey as Holly Golightly sparked a fashion frenzy when *Breakfast at Tiffany's* was released . . . and they're still as popular today. Serious Audreyites accept no imitations: made by Oliver Goldsmith, the legendary specs were re-released in 2011 to celebrate the fiftieth anniversary of the film.

63. She's a class act

Everyone who met Audrey was bowled over by her elegance, grace, humility and style. Actor Van Johnson summed up his feelings in a forthright manner: 'She's a lady. When she participates in the Academy Awards, she makes all those starlets look like tramps. Thank you for your class, Audrey . . . If anyone ever said anything derogatory about her, I'd push them in the river!'

64. Her refreshingly modern take
on love and marriage

Audrey was married twice: first to director Mel Ferrer (1954–68), then to Italian psychiatrist Andrea Dotti (1969–82), before settling down with TV actor Robert Wolders who was to be her partner for the rest of her life. 'It's a wonderful feeling to be able to not only love somebody and be loved, but to trust them,' she told Barbara Walters in 1989, adding, 'marriage is not important . . . There's no reason for marrying or not marrying.'

65. She wasn't afraid to tackle
controversial roles

In 1961 Audrey starred opposite Shirley MacLaine in *The Children's Hour* (originally released as *The Loudest Whisper* in the UK), a film dealing with the then 'shocking' topic of lesbianism. Based on the 1934 play by Lillian Hellman and directed by William Wyler, this tale of two schoolteachers accused of having a sapphic relationship was nominated for five Academy Awards, but disappeared into obscurity – before finally gaining DVD distribution decades later. The movie now stands as an LGBT classic. Surely many viewers can appreciate Shirley MacLaine's plight as she pines for the lovely Ms Hepburn! Gay or straight, male or female, it's impossible to resist her charms.

66. She was happiest
au naturel

Despite her friendship with her favourite make-up artist Alberto, Audrey actually preferred being *sans* face paint. According to another of Audrey's close friends, Doris Brynner, 'she was happiest not wearing makeup . . . at home with the dogs and the flowers and giggling away or going to the movies, not being a movie star at all, not being this idol for millions of people all over the world'.

67. She looked good in a turban

No mean feat, but Audrey rocked the look

repeatedly, both on- and off-screen.

68. She even looked good in a nun's wimple!

Is it her long graceful neck that means Audrey looks more like a beautiful swan than a swaddled Egyptian mummy in *The Nun's Story*? Or is it just proof of the old saying that 'everything suits a beauty'?

69. 'She was a healer'

Shirley MacLaine, Audrey's *Children's Hour* co-star, became a lifelong friend, saying, 'Audrey was the kind of person who, when she saw someone else suffering, tried to take the pain on herself. She was a healer. She knew how to love. You didn't have to be in constant contact with her to feel you had a friend. We always picked up right where we left off.'

70. She wasn't pious or boring

Audrey was immensely kind, but could also be funny and irreverent, as composer/conductor/musician André Previn (who conducted Audrey in *My Fair Lady*) explained: 'That extraordinary mystique of hers made you think she lived on rose petals and listened to nothing but Mozart, but it wasn't true. She was quite funny and ribald. She could tell a dirty joke. She played charades with a great sense of fun and vulgarity, and she could be quite bitchy.'

71. Her attitude to parenting

Audrey loved being a mother and wasn't in the least bit 'Hollywood mom'; no shopping trips in limos and ballgowns, no diamanté diapers. 'I didn't know my mother as anything else but my mother,' says Luca. 'I only saw her in jeans and a T-shirt.'

72. She never lost touch with her inner child

'If I'm honest, I have to tell you I still read fairytales and I like them best of all.'

73. She stood up for children everywhere

When her charity work met with resistance, Audrey had her riposte ready. 'Somebody said to me the other day, "You know, it's really senseless, what you're doing. There's always been suffering, there will always be suffering, and you're just prolonging the suffering of these children [by rescuing them]." My answer is, "Okay, then, let's start with your grandchild. Don't buy antibiotics if it gets pneumonia. Don't take it to the hospital if it has an accident." It's against life – against humanity – to think that way.'

74. She was a hiccuper

The star herself announced, 'There must be something wrong with those people who think Audrey Hepburn doesn't perspire, hiccup or sneeze, because they know that's not true. In fact, I hiccup more than most.' It's official: Audrey's a hicupper.

75. Her male co-stars

Any actor worth his salt (and all those who weren't) wanted to appear opposite her Audreyness on-screen. Try this list of big-name co-stars on for size: Sean Connery, Robert Wagner, Richard Dreyfuss, Albert Finney, Ben Gazzara, Gregory Peck, William Holden, Humphrey Bogart, Henry Fonda, Fred Astaire, Gary Cooper, Anthony Perkins, Peter Finch, Burt Lancaster, George Peppard, James Garner, Cary Grant, Rex Harrison and Peter O'Toole. Phew – it's a veritable little black book of golden-era Hollywood!

76. She spilled red wine over Cary Grant

According to Audrey, the scene in 1963 thriller *Charade* where Regina spills ice cream on Alex's suit is based on a real-life spillage; she accidentally tipped red wine over Cary Grant's suit at a dinner party.

77. 'All I want for Christmas is to make another movie with Audrey Hepburn'

These were Cary Grant's words after playing opposite Audrey in *Charade*. (Clearly he didn't mind about the red wine.) Sadly the two never managed to act together again, despite attempts to attach each other to various films.

78. She couldn't believe her salary

Audrey Hepburn's paycheque of $350,000 for the 1956 film *War and Peace* was the highest fee an actress had ever received. When notified of her record-breaking earnings, Hepburn reportedly told her agent, with customary modesty, 'I'm not worth it. It's impossible. Please don't tell anyone.'

79. She was the highest paid woman

From the late 1950s until 1968, Audrey ranked alongside Liz Taylor as
the highest paid female star in the world. Due to her immense public
appeal she sometimes even earned more than her male co-stars, for
instance in the case of Rex Harrison, who reportedly got $250,000
for *My Fair Lady*, compared to Audrey's $1 million paycheque! There's
something very pleasing about the cockney flower girl out-earning
the pompous chauvinist professor . . .

80. She appeared on nine *Life* magazine covers

Forget *People* and *Hello* – back in the day, anyone who was anyone appeared on the front of *Life*. And Audrey graced more covers of this magazine than anyone, including Marilyn Monroe, who only had seven. According to an article in *Vanity Fair*, Audrey spent a combined total of two whole years of her life shooting magazine covers: she appeared on roughly 650.

81. She really, really, *really* loved food

As befits someone who did so much to help the starving children of the world, Audrey was a passionate cook. In his book, *Audrey at Home: Memories of My Mother's Kitchen*, Luca paints a portrait of the down-to-earth woman he knew who liked nothing more than spending time in her kitchen, chatting to her family and creating culinary delights. 'I never knew Audrey Hepburn,' he writes. 'To a six-year-old, it matters little if his mother is a ballerina, a scientist, an actress, or simply a mum.' What were Audrey's favourite recipes? 'If there could be only two things in this book,' writes Luca, 'they would be spaghetti and chocolate cake.'

82. She always travelled with pasta

When off on her UNICEF trips to far-flung places, Luca explains how Audrey used to pack pasta, olive oil and Parmigiano-Reggiano cheese in her suitcase.

83. She starred in a horror movie

Though often referred to as a mystery/suspense thriller, *Wait Until Dark* (1967) has all the trappings of a classic horror story: vulnerable beauty fending off scary men – and a sinister doll. Audrey plays a blind woman who is terrorised by a trio of thugs, led by Alan Arkin, as they search for a heroin-stuffed doll. Horror-master Stephen King declared the film the scariest movie of all time in his non-fiction book, *Danse Macabre* – and he should know!

84. She has an EGOT

Only twelve artists have ever won an Emmy, a Grammy, an Oscar and a Tony – and Audrey's one of them! She won an Oscar for her regal performance in *Roman Holiday* in 1954, followed by a Tony a few weeks later for her leading performance in the play *Ondine*. She won her Emmy for the TV show *Gardens of the World with Audrey Hepburn* – which aired the day after her death in 1993 – and the Grammy for Best Spoken Word Album for Children in 1994 for *Audrey Hepburn's Enchanted Tales*. This makes her the only person to have completed her EGOT posthumously.

85. She was always learning

Or 'absorbing logic', as she called it. 'My life isn't theories and formulae. It's part instinct, part common sense. Logic is as good a word as any and I've absorbed what logic I have from everything and everyone . . . from my mother, from training as a ballet dancer, from *Vogue* magazine, from the laws of life and health and nature.'

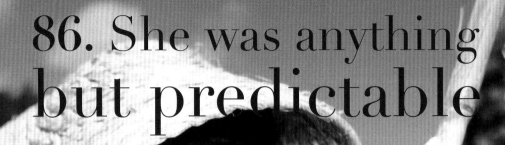

86. She was anything but predictable

In 1971, while focusing on being a full-time mother to Sean and Luca, Audrey made a series of Japanese wig commercials for a company called Varie. Her contract stated that the commercials would never appear outside Japan.

87. Her positivity

Despite the sadness in her life: abandonment by her father, the atrocities of war, her miscarriages and marriage breakups and the suffering she witnessed as a UNICEF ambassador, Audrey remained resolutely positive. 'Nothing's impossible,' she stated. 'The word itself says "I'm possible!"'

88. She never gave up on true love

Aged 51, after two marriage breakdowns, in 1980 Audrey met Robert Wolders, a Dutch actor working in the US in shows like *Laredo*, *The Man from U.N.C.L.E.* and *Bewitched*. In a strange twist of fate, Robert had grown up near Audrey in Holland during the war, so the two soulmates had experienced many of the same childhood hardships.

89. She was proud to age gracefully

'She was very proud and very happy about ageing,' says Luca. 'She really believed that women and men shouldn't hide their ageing process even by wearing youthful clothes or going too far . . . with plastic surgery because that's when it becomes ridiculous and there's an age for everything.'

90. But would never have condemned anyone who did opt for a nip or tuck

Audrey's son Sean told the *MailOnline*: 'My mother thought everybody should be allowed to make their own choices and be allowed to feel more beautiful. I don't know if she would have had surgery herself, but maybe and in her general style it would have been minor.'

91. She played Maid Marian in her forties

Long before Cate Blanchett and Russell Crowe, there was another set of 'mature' lovers in Sherwood. Audrey flew the flag for middle-aged romancers everywhere when she starred opposite Sean Connery in the 1976 feature *Robin and Marian*. The film marked a rare return to the screen for Ms Hepburn, to the delight of fans and critics alike (though the film itself received mixed reviews). Frank Thompson wrote in *American Film*, 'Hepburn's Marian is the heart of the film; for once, neither fragile nor innocent. Her performance has steel in it, and a touch of madness.'

92. She listened to her kids

Having put acting on the back burner to focus on being a mother, Audrey came out of a nine-year retirement for *Robin and Marian* – at the encouragement of her sons! Sean and Luca were big James Bond fans and convinced their mamma to sign up to work with 007 himself, Sean Connery. Audrey agreed and had her children with her on set where they learned archery, while their mother stood up for romance. She felt that the director Richard Lester sometimes put too much focus on the action side of the film. 'With all those men, I was the one who had to defend the romance in the picture. Somebody had to take care of Marian.'

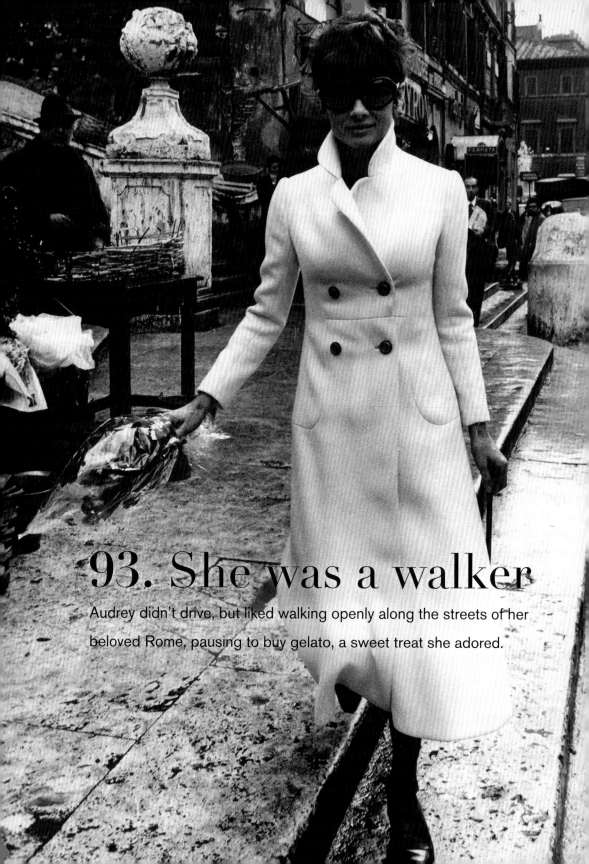

93. She was a walker

Audrey didn't drive, but liked walking openly along the streets of her beloved Rome, pausing to buy gelato, a sweet treat she adored.

94. Her one-in-a-billion voice

A mixture of Dutch inflections and British elocution lessons, Audrey's dulcet tones, complete with drawn-out vowels and sometimes unusual emphasis, defy imitation.

95. She believed that kindness can change the world

'I feel so strongly that's where it all starts – with kindness. What a different world this could be, if everyone lived by that.'

96. And that chocolate could help 'banish sadness'

At the end of the German occupation, a Dutch soldier gave Audrey seven chocolate bars, a gift she believed helped her through those final days of austerity.

97. She *is* the twentieth century

As shoe-designer to the stars Manolo Blahnik puts it, 'the imprint of Miss Hepburn is absolutely, totally present. Like it or not, she will be the most important look of the twentieth century.'

98. Her final acting role was as an angel

Appropriately, angelic Audrey made her final on-screen appearance as an angel named Hap in Steven Spielberg's 1989 movie, *Always.*

99. 'She was a dream'

Richard Dreyfuss, who acted with Audrey in *Always*, summed up her magical personality: 'She was perfectly charming and perfectly loving. She was a dream. And she was the kind of dream that you remember when you wake up smiling.'

100. Her dreams came true

'It's going to sound like a thumping bore,' Audrey told Larry King in 1991, 'but my idea of heaven is Robert and my two sons at home – I hate separations – and the dogs, a good movie, a wonderful meal and great television all coming together. I am really blissful when that happens. My goal was not to have huge luxuries. As a child, I wanted a house with a garden, which I have today. This is what I dreamed of.'

First published in 2016 by Plexus
Publishing Limited
Copyright © 2016 by Plexus
Publishing Limited
Published by Plexus Publishing Limited
The Studio, Hillgate Place,
18-20 Balham Hill,
London SW12 9ER
www.plexusbooks.com

British Library Cataloguing
in Publication Data
A catalogue record for this book is
available from the British Library

ISBN-13: 978-0-85965-530-9

Designed by Coco Balderrama
Printed in Turkey by Imago

Acknowledgements

The publisher would like to thank Joanna
Benecke for her thoughtful, illuminating
selection of reasons. In her lifetime,
Audrey Hepburn gave interviews to
an array of personalities, newspapers,
magazines and periodicals, and these have
proved invaluable in researching this
book. Thanks are due to: Barbara Walters,
Vanity Fair, *Vogue*, *Harper's Bazaar*,
Hello, *People*, *Life*, *Wall Street Journal*, the
New York Times, the *Telegraph*, the *Daily
Mail*, the *Times*, the *Guardian* and the
Independent. The following books, websites
and fan pages have also provided a unique
insight into Audrey's life and times:
*Audrey at Home: Memories of My Mother's
Kitchen*, by Luca Dotti; *Enchantment:
The Life of Audrey Hepburn*, by Donald
Spoto; *Audrey Hepburn: Fair Lady of the
Screen*, by Ian Woodward; *Audrey in Rome*,
by Luca Dotti and Ludovica Damiani;
Audrey Hepburn, Elegant Spirit, by Sean
Hepburn Ferrer; *Remembering Audrey*, by
Bob Willoughby; audreyhepburn.com;
goldderby.com; altfg.com; audrey1.org;
examiner.com; unicef.org; ahepburn.com,
YouTube.com.

Thanks to the following agencies for
supplying photographs: Paramount
Pictures/Moviepix/Getty Images; Everett/
Shutterstock/Rex Features; Movie Market;
Hulton Archive/Getty Images; John Kobal
Foundation/Moviepix/Getty Images;
UNICEF/Hulton Archive/Getty Images;
CSU Archives/Everett/Shutterstock/Rex
Features; Popperfoto/Getty Images; *New
York Daily News* Archive/Getty Images;
Michael Ochs Archives/Stringer/Moviepix/
Getty Images; 1645/Gamma-Rapho/Getty
Images; PIERLUIGI/Shutterstock/Rex
Features; George Konig/Shutterstock/Rex
Features; ullstein bild/Getty Images; Peter
Charlesworth/LightRocket/Getty Images;
RDA/Hulton Archive/Getty Images;
Paul Popper/Popperfoto/Getty Images;
Pierluigi Praturlon/Shutterstock/Rex
Features; Snap/Shutterstock/Rex Features;
Ernst Haas/Getty Images; Stringer/
Hulton Archive/Getty Images; AGF s.r.l./
Shutterstock/Rex Features; Archive
Photos/Pictorial Parade/Getty Images;
Team/Alinari/Shutterstock/Rex Features.